If You Have a Hat

by Gerald Hawksley

If you have a hat -

put it on your head.

If you have a bedbug -

tuck him up in bed.

If you have a seed -

help it grow into a flower.

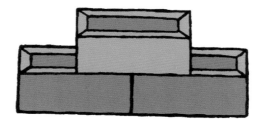

If you have some bricks -

build yourself a tower.

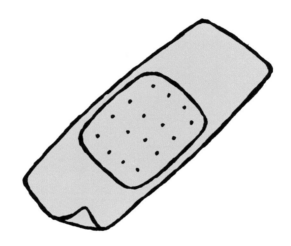

If you have a Band-Aid -

stick it on your knee.

If you have a ship -

sail it out to sea.

If you have a camera -

take a photograph.

If you have a hippo -

put him in the bath.

If you have some music -

do a little dance.

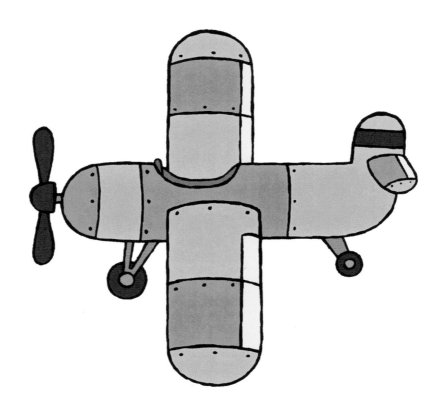

If you have an airplane -

take a trip to France.

If you have an apple -

bake it in a pie.

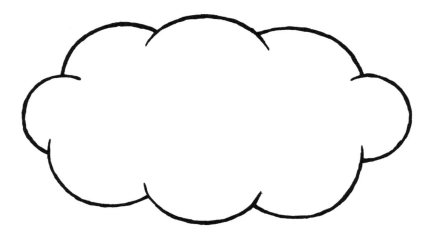

If you have a cloud -

put it in the sky.

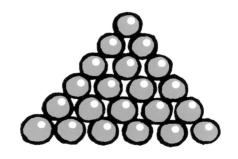

If you have some peas -

eat them off a spoon.

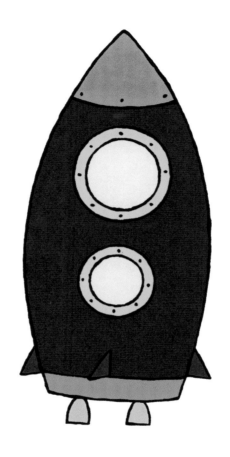

If you have a rocket -

fly it to the moon.

If you have some cheese -

give it to a mouse.

If you have a tree -

make yourself a tree house.

If you have a bicycle -

ride it in a race.

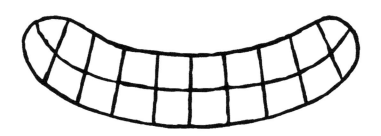

And if you have a smile -

put it on your face!

Made in the USA
Lexington, KY
16 April 2012